PSALMS DOWN-UNDER

Text by Joy Cowley
Photos by Terry Coles

Catholic Supplies (N.Z.) Ltd

Dedicated to Monsignor B. Tottman

4th printing, August 1999

ISBN 0908696-14-0

Psalms Down-under

Text © 1996 Joy Cowley

Photos © 1996 Terry Coles

© 1996 this publication, Catholic Supplies (N.Z.) Limited.

Cover and text design: Kapiti Print Media Ltd, Paraparaumu Beach,
                           New Zealand.

Printing: Lithoprint Ltd, Wellington, New Zealand.

Contents

Introduction

The popularity of *Aotearoa Psalms,* the first psalm collection from Joy Cowley and Terry Coles, has been remarkable. It has run to eight editions and sold more than 12,000 copies. Next year an edition is to be published in the United States.

What explains this publishing phenomenon at a time when New Zealanders are notably apathetic towards religion? A new survey on religious practice confirms what we all know — a shrinking number of New Zealanders is actively involved in any form of religious activity. 78% of those who describe themselves as Christians are not actively involved.

This disillusion with institutional religion, however, should not be taken as an apathy for things spiritual. The need has not gone away. People are still human, anxious to find ways to cope with soul-destroying adversity. People are still desperate that their lives have meaning, that their work makes a difference, that their relationships have substance. People still struggle to forgive and be forgiven for falling short.

We are spiritual beings, dissatisfied with the thin gruel of consumerism. We desperately seek to believe in ourselves more. Pinned to the ground, we want only to fly.

Joy Cowley and Terry Coles show us how. *Psalms Down-under* are a celebration of the human spirit alive in God's creation. They offer no easy escape to a God who will anaesthetise us against pain, but they do rejoice always in the mystery of God's presence among us.

There is nothing saccharine about *Psalms Down-under.*

> *I surrender to the mystery*
> *of loss that turns to gain.*
>
> *– Loss*

Joy Cowley's familiar colloquial voice and her character-
istically domestic view of God whose "presence in the most
ordinary things often takes me by surprise" is once again to
the fore. Parables and biblical metaphors are refreshingly
re-cast in contemporary terms:

> *God of washing,*
> *God of vacuum cleaner bags,*
> *God of sparrows, lilies and mustard seeds,*
> *my house is your tabernacle.*
>
> *– God of Washing*

Add to that a very adult awareness of the mix of good
and evil which is life for all of us, and the unsolicited
blows that strike within:

> *. . . there's been a kind of death,*
> *part of me wrapped in a shroud*
> *and buried in a tomb*
> *while the rest of me stands by*
> *wondering why the light has gone out.*
>
> *– Lazarus*

This is life lived on another level, lived so close to God
"that I can't say where I end and you begin" — a wonder-
ful liberation from the relentlessly material view of existence that so often passes for living.

For me *Psalms Down-under* conveys a clearer, more insistent Christian voice than *Aotearoa Psalms*. I am struck most by the simple eloquence of lines such as:

> *For hunger itself is the guide,*
> *the gift from God that seeks God.*
> — *Hunger*

and

> *poverty is having too much or too little*
> *of this earth's resources. Either way*
> *we become prisoner to our material wants . . .*
> — *Tzedekah*

These poems are a mature reflection on the human condition – the loss, the pain, "how corruption can occur to taint the best of intentions". The wisdom is right there under the skin of our experience.

The combination of Joy Cowley's psalms and Terry Coles' camera is once again a successful one. The images revere their down-under subjects — whether they be the grand landscape, the flower, or the spontaneous human moment of father and child.

Taken together, words and pictures unveil another world which is there for us to draw strength and inspiration from, a world located in the midst of our loss and uncertainty but "torched by the breath of God". *Psalms Down-under* is faith alive.

Michael Fitzsimons

1. Nativity

Look now!
It is happening again!
Love like a high spring tide
is swelling to fullness and overflowing
the banks of our small concerns.

And here again is the star,
that white flame of truth
blazing the way for us
through a desert of tired words.

Once more comes the music,
angel song that lifts our hearts
and tunes our ears
to the harmony of the universe,
making us wonder how
we ever could have forgotten.

And now the magi within us
gathers up gifts of gold and myrrh,
while that other part of ourselves,
the impulsive, reckless shepherd,
runs helter skelter with arms outstretched
to embrace the wonder of it all.

We have no words
to contain our praise.
We ache with awe,
we tremble with miracle,
as once again,
in the small rough stable of our lives,
Christ is born.

2. Friend

Good on you, Friend,
for being a presence of Christ to me.
You came when I needed you.
I didn't have to ask.
You didn't have to say.
You just turned up out of the blue,
carrying no luggage,
both hands free to carry mine,
and somehow, you made it look
as though I was doing you a favour
by letting you be there.

It beats me how you knew
what a burden I was bearing.
You know, I can't believe
that I talked so much
or that you could be attentive
for such a long time.
But I do know that when I left you,
the sun was shining,
a bird was singing
and there was a beautiful day
waiting to be used.

So good on you, friend, for being there,
and letting me tell my story,
and for giving to me three ways,
as a friend,
as a teacher of what friendship
is all about,
and as a channel of something
that I call holiness.

3. God of Washing

God of washing, God of unmade beds,
God of dented saucepans and worn-out brooms,
your presence in the most ordinary things
often takes me by surprise.

I listen to the morning news
and think of your presence
at a United Nations' peace conference,
at the launching of a space probe,
or in the development of a vaccine,
or the discovery of a new planet.
Then I look down and see you
winking in bubbles of detergent.

God of washing,
God of stains and missing buttons,
wherever else you might be,
you are right here with me,
defrosting and cleaning the freezer,
picking up bits of plastic toys
from the living room floor,
and each time you nudge my heart
with the warmth of your presence,
recognition leaps like a song.

I know it! Oh, I know it!

God of washing,
God of vacuum cleaner bags,
God of sparrows, lilies and mustard seeds,
my house is your tabernacle.

4. A Prayer for Discernment

God, when I was a child
the issues of right and wrong were simple,
clearly laid down as law by others.
But now that I'm an adult,
responsible for my life,
now that I must make decisions
based on my own experience,
nothing appears clear-cut any more.
Now, I see the movements of life
which can turn evil into good
and I know how corruption can occur
to taint the best of intentions.
In fact, it sometimes seems
that good and evil aren't separate at all,
but mixed in every action.
And that can make choices difficult.

Loving God,
I pray for the courage to make wise decisions.
In the security of your love,
may I step past the ignorance and fear
which makes me self-protective,
and in a multitude of choices,
may I always lean towards the greater good.

5. Hospitality

I asked Love to help me
greet the stranger in myself.
I knew how to open my door to the world
and greet everyone out there as friend
but I didn't have any kind of welcome
for the impoverished one within.
She was the weakness I couldn't acknowledge.
She was the pain I didn't allow.
She was the leper I'd tried to cast out of the city,
the one who cried at night in lonely places.
I thought that if I let her in
she'd cause me no end of trouble,
and I was afraid.

But Love helped me to prepare a feast.
We set the table, Love and I,
and then I did it,
I invited my stranger.
"Answer the door," said Love.
"You have nothing to fear."

She came in slowly.
I put my arms around her
and embraced her in her rags
and we wept together for the years of separation.
I sat my stranger at the head of the table,
gave her the best of food and wine
and, claiming her as my own,
began to introduce her to my friends.
"But who shall I say she is?"
I whispered to Love.
"I can't call her a stranger now."
Love smiled and said, "Don't you know?
She is the Christ."

6. Lazarus

I don't intend it to happen.
It just sneaks up on me
and before I know it
there's been a kind of death,
part of me wrapped in a shroud
and buried in a tomb
while the rest of me stands by
wondering why the light has gone out.
Then you, my Friend, all knowing,
seek me out and knock
at the edge of my heart,
calling me to come forth.
I argue that I can't.
Death is death and I'm too far gone
for story book miracles.
But you keep on calling,
"Come forth! Come forth!"
and the darkness is pierced
by a shaft of light
as the stone begins to move.

My Friend,
I don't know how you do it
but the tomb has become
as bright as day, as bright as love,
and life has returned.

Look at me!
I'm running out,
dropping bandages all over the place.

7.   Dads

We thank God for Dads,
for their loving,
for their gentleness,
for the way they unwrap the world
as gift to their children,
for their understanding
of jokes and laughter
and quarrels and tears,
for their fatherly example
and for the times
they also need to be Mums.

We thank God for Dads
who can be as young
as their little ones,
who can listen,
who can ask questions,
who can talk about feelings,
who can claim failure
as well as success
on the path of celebration,
who can show their children
how to find the goodness of God
in themselves and others.

We thank God for Dads
whose sons grow up knowing
that being a father
is one of the two best ideas
God ever invented.

8. Creation Dance

In the beginning, God the dancer
danced the dance of love,
filling up the emptiness
of waiting with her rhythm.
She danced out the universe,
twirled the stars and planets,
held light and dark in either hand
and clapped them into wisdom.

And everything moved in a circle of love,
a circle of love, a circle of love.
And everything moved in a circle of love
and God saw that it was good.

Then God danced the mountains up
and trod the seas deep down.
She creased the land for rivers,
made rivers to hug the land.
Everywhere her footsteps went,
the earth broke into green,
flax and fern and tree and vine,
dancing to the rhythm of love.

And everything moved in a circle of love,
a circle of love, a circle of love.
And everything moved in a circle of love
and God saw that it was good.

When the earth was filled with the music
of every kind of creature,
God danced two people into being
and named them woman and man.
She sang to them, "My children,
join me in creation.
Come and be my partners
dancing the dance of love."

And everything moved in a circle of love,
a circle of love, a circle of love.
And everything moved in a circle of love,
and God saw that it was good.

9. The Tenth Leper

Today, my God, I came back to thank you.
The other nine times I forgot.
It was not ingratitude, you understand,
but a careless enthusiasm.
I prayed for healing and when it came
I got swept away on a wave of new energy
and was so busy making up for lost time
that somehow you got left behind.

Today, my God, I remembered to come back
to the inner stillness where you waited
to share in my rejoicing. I didn't run
but returned quietly, holding out my heart
like a bowl, containing all the thanks I knew.

You accepted it with pleasure,
saying nothing about the other nine times
and the nine times before that.
Then, when you gave my heart back to me,
not empty but overflowing with your love,
I experienced yet another healing.

10. Offering

O God, I reach out to you
as a child reaches for its mother,
and like a child I offer you
a special gift of love.
It's something unique.
In all the history of the universe
there has never been another like it.
It's something of great beauty,
small and fragile, yet amazingly strong.
It has all the colours of the rainbow,
a gift of shimmering contrasts,
and I offer it exactly as it is,
without any wrapping,
because you already know it
better than I do.

So here it is, my God,
with all my love and gratitude,
the gift you made,
the gift you cherish,
the gift of me.

11. The Little Girl

Today the Spirit of God comes not as fire or wind
or a great movement on the face of the waters,
but as a little laughing girl calling us to play.
She is new, eternally young, the freshest thing there is
in a world grown old with too many winters.
Her voice shakes out all those tight buds of hope
that we thought would never blossom
and where she runs, the frost-bitten ground grows warm
and sends up flowers filled with a fragrance
we dimly remember as trust.

This little girl, this infant Shekinah
who is all innocence and knowledge of God,
can do the most amazing things in her smallness.
No, really! She can! With that laughter of hers
she can dance into the space between eye and heart,
like some song that we heard before we were born,
like a flame from a light we have always known,
and before we realise it, spring has happened,
the green season of God has happened.
Love is blossoming all over the place.

Then we realise that the whole world turns
on truth that is this joyous and simple,
and we know that we too, are eternally young.

12. Learning

Spirit of Love, you are strong and true,
a constant wind to my sail.
Your power will never fail me
but the direction I take depends
on the way I set my sail,
and that skill can only come
from practical experience of journey.
Yes, I've studied manuals, examined charts,
listened to the advice of others,
but in the end it's a matter
of getting out there and doing it.
And I can be sure that just as I think
I've got everything under control,
I tack the wrong way and capsize.
That's how it is with learning.

Spirit of Love, strong and unchanging,
you teach me that the trough of the wave
is as important as its crest.
Thank you for giving me the freedom
to learn through trial and error
and thank you for showing me
that if I don't make mistakes
I don't make anything at all.

13. The Burning Bush

I am a very small tree in a desert
and I am torched by the breath of God.
I don't ask for it. It just happens,
a suddenness inside me and then a presence
of wind and flame burning, burning,
and I cover my eyes with my fears,
knowing that I am too small and too frail
to bear this firestorm of love.

I cry out, "God, God, what are you doing?
I have always needed your Sunday warmth
but I can't cope with this searing
which feels like both heaven and hell.
You leave no part of me untouched.
That's not what I planned.
Please go away!"

There is no answer in the wind and fire,
but little by little, the blindness of my fear
is dissolved and I see with clear eyes
that the desert round me is no longer a desert.
It has all been lit by the strong flame of love,
every bush, every tree transformed beyond itself.
I am not alone in this. I never was.
Every living thing has been summoned
to be on fire with the love of God
and to turn all barren places
into sacred ground.

14. Surrender

God, I come before you
as empty as a paper cup,
waiting to be filled
with the wine of your presence.
Somewhere back along the road a bit,
I dropped all those things
I was going to offer you,
the doing, the giving, the praying.
I'll pick them up again later,
but right now,
it's just you and me, God,
and there's not much of me.
It's a good feeling
to be this empty, this open
to the amazing stillness of you,
not knowing how to name you
or the life that you pour into me.

God, right now I feel so small
and yet so vast.
I can't say where I end
and you begin.

15. Tzedekah (Justice)

God our loving Creator,
in the good news of Christ Jesus we come to you
to thank you for the gift of life
and for the wisdom of the Christian tradition
which guides us in the celebration of being.

The gospels teach us that poverty
is having too much or too little
of this earth's resources. Either way
we become prisoner to our material wants
and have our wider choices restricted.
Whether we are Lazarus or the rich young man
our material condition will limit our growth.

I thank you, God, for teaching me
to recognise where my true values lie.

We learn in the gospels the need to work for a living
in employment, and also more directly
for ourselves and for our families
in the growing and preparing of food,
the making of clothing and shelter,
creating, using, reusing, recycling,
cherishing the precious resources of this earth.

I thank you, God, for the gift of my hands
and the knowledge of the goodness of work.

Again and again, the gospels celebrate community.
We respond to the invitation
to share our lives with people,
and we offer our time and caring.
Show us how to empower and be empowered by them,
how to share knowledge and skills and build together
a tomorrow that is strong in enduring values.

I thank you, God, for the way you've enriched me
through people whose lives are different from mine.

The gospels tell us not to judge others
but to become personally involved with decisions
which work for the greater good of society.
We know the danger of becoming armchair critics,
and as we look for opportunities to take part
in the processes that shape our lives,
we ask that your strength and wisdom guide us.

I thank you, God, for the knowledge
that in Christ Jesus all things are possible.

Amen.

16. A Song of Creation

Oh, my Creator,
I can't take it in.
My mind won't wrap around it,
my breath is hushed with awe
as I consider this being you have made,
this delicate machine, this I.

I can't guess how old the universe is,
billions and billions of years,
but I do know that every element
in this body of mine, has existed
from the very beginning.
Way back, when this earth
was a ball of fire in the void,
the components of my being
were as much there with you,
as was my soul, oh God.
Every atom of me that is now,
was also then.

And I know that in the entire history
of this amazing universe,
there has never been another creation
exactly like me.
Nor will there be another me,
ever again.
I am one of a kind.

Oh God, when I think about that,
I feel faint with wonder
and gratitude.

17. Spring Cleaning

Hey, Jesus,
did you say something about possessions?
Well, it just so happens
that I'd be very pleased
if you'd take some of this stuff
which keeps getting in the way.

For example, that old trunk
filled with ideas which no longer fit.
In the past they've served me well
but now they're tight. They chafe
and are splitting at the seams.
You've given me new garments to grow into.

Over here, I've got stacks of answers
dating back to the days
when life was filled with questions.
You took the questions last collection.
I don't know why I'm hanging on to these.

Down by your feet, are some masks.
I keep accumulating those
in spite of the fact that I promised myself
I'd never wear masks again. They're so heavy!

These bundles are heavy too,
judgemental attitudes wrapped in fear.
Can you help me to move them?

Hey Jesus,
why don't I just hand it all to you
and let you deal with it?
Why don't I just stand here
and admire the results of our spring-cleaning?
You know, this house is surprisingly big.
I didn't know I had so much space.
Hey Jesus,
would you like to move in?

18. The Hidden

Everything has its roots in God.
In the greening of the tree,
the music of falling water,
the surge of the incoming tide,
the rise and fall of seaweed,
the barking of seals on a rock,
the dive of the humpback whale,
the I AM is manifest.

Everything is contained in God.
In the smoke from a driftwood fire,
the wind sharpening leaves of flax,
the shadow of trout in a moonlit stream,
the first fall of snow on the mountain,
the kingfisher flying to her nest,
the I AM is moving.

Everything speaks of God.
In the winner's shout of celebration,
the laughter round the dinner table,
the child's cry of pain in the night,
the groan of the woman in childbirth,
the sigh of the man's last breath,
the I AM is heard.

God is everything's secret.

19. The Parable of the Sower

The sower went forth to sow
and some seed fell on the wayside
and the birds came and ate it.
But the sower went on sowing
and the next time round
the birds were not there
and the barren wayside blossomed.

Some of the seed fell on stony soil.
It sprang up but the sun burnt it
and it withered away to nothing.
But the sower went on sowing
and the next time it was raining
and the stony wilderness
produced a fine harvest.

Some of the seed fell amongst thistles
which grew up through it and choked it,
but the sower went on sowing
and in time the thistles decayed
to form compost for another lot of seed
which grew in soil made richer
for having had weeds in it.

Some seed fell on fertile ground
and gave a good harvest
first time round, and that was fine,
but it made no difference to the sower
who owned all land with equal love,
the wayside, the stones, the thistle patch,
no less than the fertile ground,
who tended each one in its season
and according to its need,
so that each, in its own right time,
produced an abundant crop.

And the sower goes on sowing.

20. Tension

I am being pulled two ways.

There is a voice in my heart
which calls me to journey
out there in deep waters,
while another voice in my head
tells me to stay close
to a safe and familiar shore.

The heart voice is like a strong tide
drawing me to the infinite.
The head voice moors me
to a secure harbour
of possessions and ideas.

I know that the head voice
comes from my human nature
and is a part of my instinct
for survival on this planet.
The voice is loud, and says
in a number of different ways,
"What about me? What about me?"

The voice of the heart is gentle
and as quiet as moonlight.
All that it says is, "Come!"
but its pull is very strong
and my heart strains away from my head
in deep longing.

I know that there is a season
for waiting in safe harbours,
a time for material security,
for feeding the human self
with things and ideas of things.
What I pray for in this moment
is the gift of discernment.
May I learn to read the tide, and know
when to cast off the moorings
to sail those deep and uncharted waters
of God's infinite love.

21. Worship

We step out of our every day selves
and into this cathedral
of sky and earth and sea
where all the parables of life
are played out in their seasons
and all the seasons held as one
in the love of God.

Everything here is holy in its being.
Every fern, tree, rock, drop of sea,
exists as a prayer of thanksgiving,
and together they speak a chapter
in the gospel of wonder
which is laid upon our lives.

Eagerly our hearts lean forward,
to listen to the praise of tree ferns
echoing in the still water,
and to see the shimmering of the divine
behind the surface of each leaf.

Look! It is everywhere!
The love of the creator glowing
in mountains and in ocean,
in pebble and stem, fish and bird,
and us! Yes, yes! The light of God in us!

For we too, are sacred.
We too, are named holy.
And the meaning of our lives
is thanksgiving.

22. Smallness

God of endless galaxies
you come to me in the smallest space
of my existence, the child space,
and as often as I claim my littleness
you meet me with an eagerness of giving.

I receive the jewel of your presence
in the detail of the moment,
God in the dew on a cobweb,
God in the notes of a bellbird,
God in the curve of a fern frond
and the shining path of a snail.

Love that cannot be measured,
when you hold me in my smallness,
a gentleness encloses me,
as soft as a sparrow's wing,
and healing drops like a feather
on my wounded heart
and in a song-filled instant,
life becomes simple again.

God, God,
help me to protect my smallness,
for there is within me
a disciple who is impressed
by big and powerful things
and that disciple always tries
to send the little child away.

Knowing my smallness
is knowing the kingdom of heaven.

23. Hunger

The sign outside the cafe said,
"Be guided by your hunger."
We looked at each other, you and I,

picking up the parable,
thinking of all the times
we had misread spiritual hunger
and had unsatisfactory meals.
The world, it seems, is full of diets,
should and shouldn't, do and don't,
accompanied by pressured sales talk.
At times it has been hard to know
how to best nurture the soul
and in an absence of decision,
our inner selves have starved.

"Be guided by your hunger."
The truth is always simple.
For hunger itself is the guide,
the gift from God that seeks God.
It will turn us from food too weak for us,
and likewise from food too strong,
and bring us to what is right
for our present stage of development.

We will be guided by our hunger
and whatever tastes good to the soul,
will be the feast of God.

24. Loss

Somethings's dead inside me.
Some yesterday is slain.
My heart is hung upon a cross,
My thoughts are dull with pain.
And yet there is within me
a hope I can't explain.

For in the darkness I can see
God dancing in the rain.

I surrender to the mystery
of loss that turns to gain.
The little seed of wheat must die
to become a field of grain,
and I know it's in this time of grief,
that Christ is risen again.

For in the darkness I can see
God dancing in the rain.

25. Stones

Today I came to a shining beach
covered with a litany of stones:
gravel, pebbles, boulders, many colours,
each one like a word of praise
and the whole, a triumphant song.

As I picked up stones at random,
feeling their skin against mine,
and absorbing the loveliness of them,
I thought that I was a bit like that beach,
with every stone a gesture of love
from a person who'd cared about me
at some time in my life.
From the moment of conception,
when God spoke and I was,
love has shaped my being
and the givers are still with me,
contained within their gifts,
people who've laid a litany of loving,
stone by stone, word by word, touch by touch,
showing me the truth of my existence.

For a long time I sat on that beach,
adding to its song, my own gratitude,
and when I shut my eyes and tried to imagine
what the beach would look like
without all those shining stones,
I understood in a new and deeper way,
the meaning of my life as gift.

26. Morning

God, I am awake, this I.
My eyes are open.
My heart beats. My lungs work.
Here and now I have
this sacred gift of me
which is about to unwrap
a second gift,
the gift of a bright new day.

I see the day before me, fresh,
untouched by yesterday
and free of tomorrow.
Will it also become sacred
with my unwrapping?

God, may I receive all of the gift
of this bright new day
without judgement or prejudice.
May my vision be clear enough
to see beauty in everything.
May I greet each moment
in its uniqueness and say thank you
for opportunities to learn.
And God, may I not forget to give
the child in me some space to sing
and dance with all the little miracles
that announce your presence.

If it so happens
that I am clumsy in the unwrapping,
if I drop or break something,
then remind me, God,
to be gentle with myself.

There will be another gift tomorrow.

27. Jesus said: I am the Way, the Truth and the Life.

You are the Way.
You are the bridge between earth and heaven,
between the smallness of self
and the greatness of God.
You are the path we follow
and can never lose
because it lies in our hearts.
You are the mountain, the valley,
the rough and the smooth.

You are all points of the compass.
Whoever or wherever we are,
you hold our journey in yours.

You are the Truth.
You have planted your truth within us,
the same truth for all people.
Each of us is a different container
and we wrap you in different ways
according to our culture
and our customs of worship,
but in our diversity
you are our common language
and when we meet you in each other
there is recognition and rejoicing,
for truth always knows truth.

You are the Life
and there is no life without you
for you are the substance
and breath of all things.
Your life grows within and around us,
the movement of sap in our seasons,
the ebb and flow of our tides.
You are the living
and the knowing of living
which we carry with us
through the doorway of death.

You who are the Way,
the Truth and the Life,
gift us with the vision
to always see you in all things.

28. Comfort

I admit it, God!
I'm addicted to comfort.
I have to confess that most of my prayer
is for an easy path for myself and others,
a pleasant path that's not too steep,
with the right mixture of lights and shade,

plenty of shelter on the way
and, of course, the right companions.

When these come to me, I thank you,
all the time quietly feeling
that I've done something to deserve them.
But if I find an obstacle in my path,
I don't own it or see it as your gift,
but reject it as some kind of enemy
and cry out for you to remove it.

But now, looking back on the obstacles
which have been major gifts in disguise,
I thank you for all the times
you have answered my prayer
by giving not what I wanted
but what I needed.

Loving God, I praise you for all of the journey
and the way you give with two hands —
ease and discomfort, rough and smooth,
all part of a oneness of progress.
Those things dropped across my path
when I needed to be brought to a stop
and to a stillness.

Obstacles make me stronger.
They challenge me to use
the resources you have given me.
But most important of all,
they make me think about who I am,
who you are, Creator God,
and what this journey is all about.

29. Prayer

I think it's kind of funny
that we have only one word for prayer,
when we come to God in so many ways.

Sometimes,
There is the barn-storming prayer,
the hammering on the door,
the cry of pain or anger
from a desperate grief
demanding answers.

Then there is the prayer for others,
a leaning of the heart
towards those in trouble,
a plea that God will draw them
out of their distress.

There is the prayer of doubt,
the expression of disbelief
throwing off outgrown ideas
so that we can see who we really are
and the closeness of God's love.

There is the prayer of ashes,
the cry for forgiveness,
accompanied by the relief of truth
and the freedom to put burdens
down at the side of the road..

There is the prayer of celebration,
a festive prayer adorned
with all kinds of Hallelujahs,
gratitude waved like a banner
from a thank you heart.

There is the prayer for guidance,
for sign-posts along the way
to help us understand our giftedness
and the steps we need to take
on our journey to God.

There is the prayer of community,
words of a loved tradition
falling on us in familiar notes,
and drawing us into the sacrament
of a faith given and shared.

There is the prayer of awe,
when we stand in the presence
of the intelligence of the universe,
God powerful in distant galaxies
and in every cell of our being.

There is the prayer of conversation,
the every day talk to God our friend
who helps to wash the dishes
and change the punctured tyre,
who is never too big for the detail of lives.

There is the prayer of quiet,
in that deep well of inner silence
when nothing happens
and everything happens
and we are wholly renewed.

Then there is the nameless prayer,
the prayer of God that comes in stealth
to overwhelm the heart with sweetness
and leave us with the knowledge
of the love that holds us
and goes on holding us,
however we pray
or forget to pray.

30. A Prayer for Healing

Jesus, I need healing.
At times I have a Judas voice
which betrays the Christ in me and others.
There is also a Pontius Pilate who will shrug
and walk away from the suffering in the world,
a Peter who panics and denies the truth.
Jesus, the scenes of your trial and crucifixion
get acted out in me, time after time,
and there are days when I find it hard
to look at myself in the mirror.
I need you to remind me
that forgiveness begins with self.
Life is a journey of contrasts.
It is light which makes shadows,
hills which cause valleys,
and it is your life in me
which makes me so aware
of the beauty and frailty of being human.
Jesus, show me how to be gentle
with myself, how to repair with love,
the damage I do to myself and others.
And in my moments of despair,
draw me back to your Easter message —
that there can be no resurrections
without crucifixions.

31. Good Friday

We do not call it Bad Friday
although, for the One who lived and died
the torture of that day
there would have been nothing good about it.
It was death by dishonour,
death by a pain so severe
that it filled all the spaces of thinking,
wrenching forth the cry,
"My God! My God! Why have you forsaken me!"

This One, this Christ who used nature
to descibe eternal truths,
who spoke of the cycle of the seasons
with images of grains of wheat,
fields, lilies, sparrows, grapes, figs,
fishes, sheep and flowing water,
this One was too steeped in agony
to remember that even the rarest flower
must die to produce a seeding.

But we who bear the gift
of his life and death and life,
call it Good Friday
and carry with us
the knowledge that in Him,
all of our crucifixions
are but resurrections unborn.

32. The Paschal Way

You said that if I walked your path with you
I would experience the blossoming of heaven.
I thought that you meant flowers,
blooms of celebration strewn
along the Hosanna road,
or arranged by flickering candles
in a church filled with peace,

or clustered fragrant in a heart
made into permanent summer by prayer,
or handed to me by friends
who valued flowers as much as I did.

You said that if I walked your path with you
I would discover the sweetness of God
and I expected to be given flowers.
But actually you were talking of thorns
and a cross on the road to dying
and hands and feet pierced by a truth
that I did not want to own
and a feeling of forsakeness
and a letting go
and a love so terrible it came
like a sword in my struggling heart
and finally, nothing but you and I
in the silence of the tomb.

You asked me to walk your path with you
and yes, you did mean flowers
but not the fragile things of a day.
Something of permanent fragrance
and a beauty that can't be measured
by a panacea of small comforts.
You were talking of the tomb transformed,
imprisonment into freedom,
crosses into wisdom,
suffering into compassion,
darkness into light.
You were talking of your presence,
in a life made larger by your Easter Journey.
You were talking of resurrections without end.

33. Easterings

Every hour of every day there are crucifixions,
the Christ on trial in someone, somewhere,
judged in fear, condemned in ignorance,
mocked and beaten, imprisoned, killed,
while we watch at the foot of the cross
or from three cock crows away, and ask,
"God, God, why have you forsaken them?"

The world is full of Good Fridays and Golgothas.
In the small arena of our lives,
there appears to be the same defeat of goodness
and it's difficult to wear a bright smile
when the heart hangs heavy in a darkness
full of thorns and nails and swords.
Unable to see beyond dyings, we cry,
"God, God, why have you forsaken us?"

Then something happens. Easter Sunday happens.
This movement within, this turning, breaking,
this earthquake shift through an old fault line.
A cosmic birth happens, darkness to light,
God dancing on pierced feet to make celebration
of all our dyings, even the little ones,
so that we can see, this side of the tomb,
that there are no endings, only transformations,
as we grow towards the source of our being.

In that moment of knowing, we see all of life
wrapped up in the wholeness of Easter,
and in awe we silently pray,
"God, God, you have never forsaken us."

34. Easter Sunday

This is the day of festival
and we thank you, O God of celebration,
with hymns of praise rising like balloons
and banners of love waving from our hearts.
Today we dance with the angels
round all the empty tombs in our lives,
celebrating transformation,
from grief to laughter,
from darkness into light.
Today we glimpse the truth
of suffering and death
as we move with you in your Jesus song
of resurrections without end.

35. Journey

(a reflection for a mature marriage)

Partner, we bring to each other
not spring blossom but summer fruit
ripened by experience
and made all the sweeter
by our knowledge of winter and spring.

We have known the seasons of abundance
and the times of storm and drought.
We have come through the pains of growing
to understand that petals fall
to make way for something greater,
something that was meant to be
by God, from the beginning.

Partner, I love what we have become
and what we are now for each other.
Let us go on together, you and I,
love to love, touch to touch,
to share the wisdom of autumn
and the new spring which awaits us
in the heart of winter.

36. On the Death of a Child

The beautiful soul clung to God.
"I don't want to go back!" it said.
"My road to you has been long
and difficult, and now that I am home,
I can't bear to leave you again."

God said gently, "Beautiful soul
you have indeed arrived
but for those like yourself,
who have achieved perfection,

there must always be
a short journey back
to take to those on earth,
a special gift from me."

The beautiful soul cried,
"But if I leave you,
I will forget you
and all over again
I will know the darkness
of separation."

"No," said God,
"that will not happen.
For I will come with you,
shining in your heart,
reminding you of home.
Fear not, beautiful soul.
It is only for a short time
and the parents I choose for you
will be worthy of the blessing
you bring them."

"Will they be sad when I leave?"
asked the beautiful soul.

"Yes," said God. "They will be sad.
But in a very brief span
you will give them more love
and knowledge of love
than they could otherwise find
in their lifetime of searching."

37. Learning to Fly

The walls of birth and death
were too high for me to see over
and I didn't know that my heart had wings.
As I hammered on those walls,
demanding to know their meaning,
I was aware that there was something inside me
cramped up, waiting to be unfurled,

and I could feel against my heart,
a need that was deeper than instinct,
to fly above my own questions.
But my wings were well hidden.
They needed Love to release them,
the breath of Love to shake them free of fear,
and that took time.

Knowledge of those wings, came slowly.
Taught by Love and held by Love,
my heart began to fly a little at a time,
just enough to know that flying was possible
and that a higher vision did exist
somewhere beyond me.

Then came the day of Love's surprise.
Love swept my heart up and away,
far above the walls of birth and death,
to a point that was beyond time.
And from that distance I discovered,
that birth and death were not walls at all
but little ripples coming and going,
on an eternal sea that has
neither beginning nor end.

In that moment I saw
that the meaning of birth is forgetting,
the meaning of death is remembering,
the meaning of life is growth
and the meaning of the eternal sea
which holds everything in its embrace,
is Love.

38. Grace Before Meals

The food we have here is a gift
of air and earth and sea.
As we eat it, we take on
their life and energy.
Thank you, air.
Thank you, earth.
Thank you, sea.
Thank you, Thou,
who gives all three.

Life is for living.
Love is for giving.
Friends are for caring.
Food is for sharing.
For food, friends, life and love,
and for your life in us,
Oh God, we thank you.

O thou great Giver of all things,
give us grateful hearts.

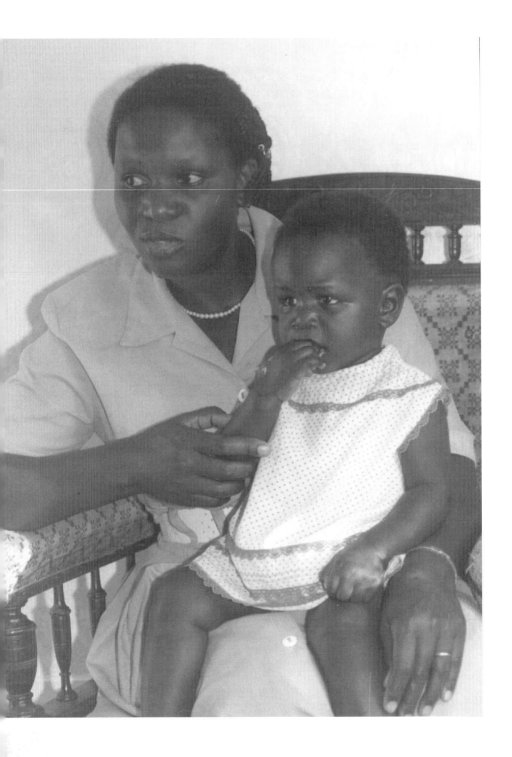

39. Virgin Birth

We have within us a virgin place,
a holy space which belongs to God alone.
We know it by its hunger,
we name it by its need,
the space which will not be touched
by the people we love
or the things we gather
or the positions we hold.

We have within us a growing place,
an eternal space that exists for Truth,
where the love of God overcomes us,
where the life of God fills us,
the Emmanuel space where we conceive
and become pregnant of the Holy One
and day by day, give birth
to Christ in the world.

40. Sacrament of the Seasons

Jesus comes to me as a springtime tree
And I receive Him as a springtime tree.
Fragrant the blossoming of the child,
Fresh with laughter, free and wild,
Carrying the green of summer.

Jesus comes to me as a summer tree
And I receive Him as a summer tree.
Warm in the sun and richly laid
With patterns of growth through light and shade,
Carrying the fire of autumn.

Jesus comes to me as an autumn tree
And I receive Him as an autumn tree.
Season of ripeness, brightly ablaze
Like a torch in the quietness of closing days,
Carrying the wood of winter.

Jesus comes to me as a winter tree
And I receive Him as a winter tree.
Gentle the cross and gentle the snow,
Gentle the path where He and I go,
Carrying the buds of spring.

41. Beauty

Oh God,
I seek a deeper awareness of beauty,
not just the attractions laid down
by my own preferences
but the true beauty of all things,
especially those I have dismissed
as unpleasant, threatening or ugly.

For when I leave myself behind
to appreciate the true beauty of the other,
I am drawn to love the other
and with love comes compassion,
the gift of seeing backwards
from the other's point of view.

Who knows?
From that position I may discover
the true beauty of myself.

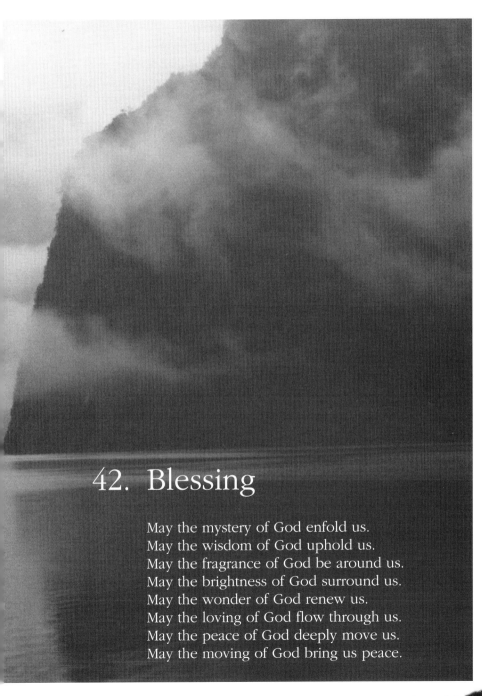

42. Blessing

May the mystery of God enfold us.
May the wisdom of God uphold us.
May the fragrance of God be around us.
May the brightness of God surround us.
May the wonder of God renew us.
May the loving of God flow through us.
May the peace of God deeply move us.
May the moving of God bring us peace.

43. The Giving

With such eagerness we carry our gifts towards the place of the newborn King. Look at us! We are like guests hurrying to a wedding, and I cannot help but note that my golden gift is as large and as finely wrapped as any I have seen.

At a point in the road, not far from the stable, I am stopped by an angel who wants to know what I am carrying. She is tall, quite stern, a security guard, I suppose. It pleases me to tell her that the package contains the treasure of a lifetime to be given to the Holy One.

"Open it," she says.

"What? Do you know how long it took me to wrap this? Or what the wrapping cost? If you're an angel, you'll already know the contents."

"Open the parcel," she says, folding her arms and firmly straddling the path.

I am reluctant but have no choice. Still, once the wrapping is removed, there are some fine treasures to display. I point them out to her. A lifetime of regular church attendance. Tithing for the poor.

Hours spent visiting the sick and comforting the bereaved. A mountain of cakes baked for fundraising stalls. Letters to the newspaper on moral issues. Marches for peaces, for justice, for the right to live. No one could be ashamed of such gifts. They are indeed fit for a king.

There is no expression on the angel's face. She looks at each in turn and says, "What else have you got?"

"What do you mean — what else?" I am angry at her lack of enthusiasm. "Do you realise what sacrifice went into these?"

"He does not need sacrifice," she says."Come now. There must be another gift."

I hesitate. "Well, yes, there is. But what I have just shown you is my finest gold. The frankincense — if I can call it that — is quite ordinary, hardly fit for the occasion."

"Let me see it."

With some embarrassment, I take from my luggage a plainly wrapped parcel, hastily tied with gardening twine. It is clumsily put together and when I pull the string, the contents spill out over the path. Nothing spectacular. A sandcastle built with one of the children. A blackened saucepan from the birthday dinner that miraculously survived a small fire. Toast crumbs, teaspoons, a teddy bear and a small tractor found when making the big bed. Silly ghost stories told on the beach under a full moon. Patti at her first communion, wanting to know how Jesus got from her stomach into her heart. The holiday the tent fell down. The pear tree we planted on the grave of a pet mouse.

The angel seems interested. She looks closely at everything and smiles. Then she picks up four shoes and a bottle of fragrant oil. "What about these?"

My embarrassment intensifies. "My husband and I — we — we massage each other's feet."

The angel gently puts them back. "Beautiful," she says. "All of it beautiful gift." She stands tall again and looks at me with clear eyes that seem as deep as forever. "Now for the third package."

I shake my head. "I'm sorry. There is no third gift."

Everyone has myrrh to offer," she says.

"Not I. Myrrh is the bitter herb of death. It has not been a part of my experience. You see, I have been extraordinarily lucky. I don't seem to have the problems that plague other poor souls. My life has been just one blessing after another."

"Myrrh is the herb of death — and resurrection," said the angel. "It is necessary for Advent journey. Without it the stable is empty."

I don't understand what she's talking about. "Sorry," I repeat. "Gold and frankincense, yes, but myrrh, no. Now will you please stand aside and let me pass?"

"Why don't we look?" says the angel, indicating my luggage.

"All right, then. Look!" I throw it open at her feet. "See? Not a drop of myrrh in sight!"

"What's this?" she says.

"What's what?"

She is pointing to a half-hidden bundle wrapped in stained newspaper.

"I don't know. I haven't seen it before. It must belong to some-one else." But as I say it, my stomach clenches and my skin turns cold.

"Open it," says the angel.

I step back, "No. I can't. It's not — not mine —"

"You know you must open it," the angel insists, and her voice is soft.

My hands shake as I pick up the package and begin the un-wrapping. Yes, it is all here. I thought I had forgotten these things, or put them away forever, but no, they are present and as alive as ever. The childhood cries that went unheard. The playground taunts. The teacher who disliked me. The struggles and rejections.

The pain wells up as real now as it was then, and my vision becomes blurred. I want to put the parcel down.

"Please continue," says the angel.

I already know what will be in the next layer. The hurt of the child within the adult. Bereavements. Losses. Failures. Feelings of inadequacy. Criticisms I could not handle. Recurring nightmares. Unspoken fears.

I am crying now, and I can't go on. "How can you call it gift!" I shout at the angel."It's all so — so ugly!"

"No, no!" she says. "It is all unborn resurrection, and resurrec-tion is the beauty of God!"

The next layer is worse. It reveals all the hurts I have inflicted on others, from careless gossip to deliberate betrayals. There are angry words that could not be taken back, judgements that shut out people who did not share my beliefs or lifestyle. Arrogance. Intolerance. Condescension.

I sit down in the middle of the path.

"Come," said the angel. "There is only a little more."

But she is wrong. There is no more. The last layer of wrapping reveals nothing but darkness. Every part of my life has been surrendered and now there is simply this tomb, this emptiness.

"You are very close," the angel says.

I don't reply for I am lost in the darkness. But wait! In the depth of the night, I discover a light that grows as I gaze at it.

"What do you see?" the angel asks.

The light is increasing and seems to be a living presence. My heart rises like a phoenix. "It's — it is — a star!"

"The truth of myrrh," said the angel. "Keep looking."

The light expands to fill my being with a beauty that is both as new and as old as eternity. How could I have not known this? I gaze in wonder, hushed with awe. For there, in the centre of all its brilliance, is the newborn Christ.

✳